MW01030309

The Handbook of Psychic Cold Reading

By Dantalion Jones
Author of

Perfected Mind Control – The Unauthorized Black Book Of Hypnotic Mind Control

Mind Control 101 – How To Influence the Thoughts and Minds of Others Without Them Knowing or Caring

The Forbidden Book Of Getting What You Want

Cult Control – The Building of a Cult

Mind Control Language Patterns

Mind Control Hypnosis

The Delta Success Programming CD series

The Handbook of Psychic Cold Reading

Copyright Dantalion Jones 2010

ISBN - 978-0-578-04464-4

Handbook Of Psychic Cold Reading

by Dantalion Jones

Also the author of...

"Mind Control Language Patterns"

"Mind Control Hypnosis"

"Perfected Mind Control: The Unauthorized Black Book Of Hypnotic Mind Control"

"Mind Control 101: How to Influence the Thoughts and Actions of Others Without Them Knowing or Caring"

"The Forbidden Book of Getting What You Want"

"Cult Control"

All available at amazon.com

Other Products by Dantalion Jones:

The Delta Success Program

The Handbook Of Psychic Cold Reading

Table of Contents

Dedication

To my faithful djinn, familiar and constant companion, Dantalion, the seventy-first spirit of the Goetia. "His Office is to teach all Arts and Sciences unto any, and to declare the Secret Counsel of any one; for he knoweth the Thoughts of all Men and Women, and can change them at his Will. He can cause Love, and show the Similitude of any person, and show the same by a Vision, let them be in what part of the World they Will."

Introduction

Amid all I've learned studying the human mind throughout my life the fields that have never ceased to fascinate me are persuasion and psychic "cold" reading.

For the uninitiated, a cold reading happens when you are doing a psychic reading "cold," and without knowing anything about the person.

I've already written plenty on persuasion, influence, and mind control, but now I get to pursue the art of cold reading.

If you've ever been to a psychic and walked out of the reading in a glassy eyed state of awe then you know the impact of a powerful cold reading. It is as if someone looked at you like an open book and read you page by page. What is even more fun is to know that you can give the same type of reading for others whether or not you have psychic ability.

We're talking about the art called "cold reading," but for the public at large they will simply refer to you as a psychic.

Let me say that in truth learning the art of cold reading is much like learning to play the guitar; you can do a lot just by learning the basics, and there is no end to the depth of what you can learn if you continue your studies. Like learning the guitar, you can learn the basic chords and be quite successful and entertaining, or you can begin to study and practice the most advanced, detailed, and 'classical' methods to add to your proficiency.

I can truthfully say that with a very few meager skills of cold reading (and an extreme sense of daring) I've been able to impress and entertain groups of people for hours. Think of what is possible when you learn all that you can about cold reading!

The goal of this book, at the very least, is to give you a very basic beginning and many good tricks, tips, and pointers that will will make you look as psychic as any turban-wearing palm reader. I intend to give you enough useful information to go out and start reading palms, auras and cards with just a few short hours of study. Unlike most other cold reading systems I've also put in a very simple memory system that will make learning quick, easy, and fun.

You Don't Need To Be Psychic

It's true. To sound like a psychic, and even to get paid as a psychic, you don't have to be psychic. I've done it and I've taught other people to do it too.

I can imagine the vast range of emotional responses that statement might elicit from different types of people. Let me give you an idea of the types of responses I mean.

The cynical skeptic might find this book as proof that there is no such thing as psychic abilities. **The cynical skeptic** might learn the skills in this book and us them so that at the end of a reading he could make the other person as cynical and skeptical as he is. In so doing he could set back and bask in his self righteous superiority and believe he did the world a favor by destroying someone's dream.

The angry believer, being fully convinced in the truth of psychic phenomenon, might think this book sets out to disprove psychic ability. Instead, they could have chosen to read this book in order to sharpen their skills of delivery and make themselves a better reader.

The pious do-gooder could easily assume that I am encouraging people to con, fool and scam others out of their money and ruin their faith in humanity.

If you are reading this book with any of these aforementioned predispositions then it is recommended that you return the book at once, because you are surely missing the point.

The fact is that humans can be as amazing as they are annoying, and given an open mind and the right perspective anyone can learn these skills to help people and to improve their lives. That is my only hope.

Yes, you **CAN** be a "non-psychic psychic cold reader" and actually make people feel **better** than before they met you. Many psychics who consider themselves "real" use fear, doom and gloom to hook people into their reading service. To those people I have two words: "Bad Psychic!"

To avoid any problems doing readings (whether you have a sixth sense or not) it's always highly recommended that you let people know that what you do is for entertainment ONLY. Let's face it. You're going to have more fun and last much longer as a cold reader if people feel good after they worked with you. Please keep in mind that one of your primary goals as a reader is to help people feel good.

What is a "Psychic" Cold Reading?

In my early studies of the mind and before I started to apply my studies professionally I was manning a booth at a local fair.

I had witnessed a strange older lady wandering around from booth to booth talking intently to the attendants and occasionally leaving with product. Finally she found her way to my booth. She looked intently into my eyes and told me "I think you are a good person. I want to give you a reading."

She then began to tell me how I've worked very hard and how my life has been difficult with many challenges but I've managed to persevere. She expressed to me that I had abilities that would allow me to go very far in life and that, in the end, my I will live a full and happy life.

All of what she said was very pleasing to me ... until she asked me for a donation for the reading.

That was my first experience with cold reading.

Cold reading refers to the act of telling things about someone in such away that it appears to come from "psychic" abilities.

There is nothing psychic about psychic cold reading. it is strictly a skill that combines very generalized statements that most people will agree to, the ability to read people at a glance, and a few tricks of guile.

As the title suggests, the purpose of this book is to provide a handbook that will get you started in the area of doing "psychic" cold readings for entertainment purposes. The system you'll learn here is quite simple and easy. At the same time you'll create a foundation upon which you can expand into many areas of psychic reading. You will find there is a lot of additional support material as well. Don't get overwhelmed. All that is in this book is useful and doesn't have to be learned or applied at once. Remember that it's like learning to play the guitar, and even just the basics are good enough to be entertaining.

What you'll learn here is Cold Reading **for entertainment purposes only**.

You could apply this skill to earn money doing serious reading with people who come to you to help them with their problems, but that isn't the purpose of this handbook. Instead it's best to start learning this skill for fun, to meet new people, and get to know them on a deeper level. By the way, when meeting people was my ambition I coaxed a friend to introduce me at parties as his friend, the psychic. The results were very fruitful evenings for both of us.

One use of these skills that has been put to effect quite well is in fund raising for non-profit organizations.

A few years ago I came across a ballet school that raised money once a year by setting up a "gypsy wagon" booth at a city fair. The mothers of the students agreed to learn cold reading to help earn the school some income. It was quite a sight. The ballet students, mostly young girls, would dress up in gypsy garb and call people in to get their palms, cards and auras read. Everyone knew it was all for fun and lots of fun was certainly had.

In one day the ballet school earned $1000.

To do this gypsy wagon event they all took a short two hour class in psychic cold reading, proving that the basics of cold reading can be learned in a very short time.

You can also apply the skill of psychic cold reading to work at parties and corporate events where you would be hired as entertainment.

Many use skill to meet new people. A few wise men have found that women *love* to have their palm read and to be given psychic readings. These men end up having very active lives operating in social circles where beautiful women eagerly introduce them to other beautiful women. Need I say more?

So it's from here that you'll learn the basics of cold reading. This book is designed so that if you are in any of these situations you can quickly flip through the pages and find out what you need to know.

But I think I've made it even easier than that. I've designed a memory system so that learning the basics is quick and easy. In the event that you don't yet have all the cold reading skills memorized you'll discover that there is no shame in simply saying, "I've just learned palmistry so please bare with me." You'll find that people are both forgiving and eager to get whatever insight you can provide through the use of your cold reading skills.

What Does a Cold Reading Sound Like?

Many people have the expectation that during a psychic cold reading they will sit quietly and the reader will talk without interruption about them and reveal endless details about every aspect of the their life, and especially their future.

This is seldom what happens. More often it is a conversation between the psychic and the sitter. The psychic will read the cards, palm, aura, etc. and offer impressions and interpretations of the information, and more often than not the sitter will become engaged in the process by asking questions. Even though one may anticipate hearing about their future it is more likely that the reading will mostly consist of telling the sitter about his or her character. This may be how they respond under stress, the types of people they are attracted to or should be attracted to, their basic interests and the like. Note that none of these topics are about the future, but when you are able to describe a few of these characteristics accurately (enough) then anything you say about the future will be easily accepted as true.

> Let's remember how one of history's greatest psychics would operate, The Oracle of Delphi. The Oracle of Delphi was usually a young girl who would put herself in a trance and be asked questions to predict the future or recommend courses of action.
>
> Usually her responses were incoherent gibberish that had to be interpreted by the Priest of Delphi...for a fee.

To keep the reading warm and upbeat there is a very simple mind trick the cold reader can do when meeting the subject or sitter for the first time. The reader will greet the sitter as if they were a long lost childhood friend that they haven't seen in years. This is a very sincere and warm greeting that anyone would respond to positively. To do so just imagine the feeling of joy at meeting this long lost friend (even if you've never met them before), and this alone will help to set a comfortable and positive mood for the reading.

Often the reader will then follow by asking, "Is there an area that you would like to focus on, or would you simply like a general reading?" This question does several things for the reader and the sitter. If the reader does set a specific topic of interest it tells the reader where they might focus. Even if the reading proceeds like it were a general reading, by asking the question the sitter believes they will get the answers in that particular area of interest.

The reading will then cover several topics: Love, Money, Career, Health, Travel, etc.

During the reading it will more than likely become a discussion and with the sitter speaking as much or more so than the reader.

The reader may begin with one form of reading, numerology or card reading, and then progress or intersperse it with the reading of the sitter's aura.

One cold reader I knew shared with me a very unique way of concluding each reading. He was very well practiced and at the end of the readings that went particularly well he would ask, "On a scale of one to ten how accurate do you feel the reading was?" More often than not he would be scored at an eight, nine or ten. This would have a very interesting effect on the sitter. By openly stating the accuracy of the reading they stick it in their minds that the reading went well.

If you really want to hear what a psychic reading

sounds like you can go to any search engine and type in "online psychic radio" and see what's offered. Here are a few I've listened to:

http://www.psychiconair.com

http://radiotime.com/genre/c_293/Psychic.aspx

http://www.hayhouseradio.com

There are plenty of others.

Special thanks to Roland Blade for having sent me this. His web site is http://coldreadingtechniques.blogspot.com

Your Greatest Learned Skill

One of the best skills a psychic can learn is the process of non-stop "psychic" chatter. This is done by many psychics who simply begin to speak making observations, descriptions and predictions in such a rapid fire fashion that it would be impossible for a normal person to sit and remember it in any detail. However, they **WILL** remember the things you say that are accurate.

If you have mastered non-stop psychic chatter you can begin to put in all the aspects of cold reading that you will learn here as well.

The best way to learn to do this is to simply start doing it. Set aside some time alone to imagine sitting with a client and simply begin talking, making every effort to sound like any psychic you've ever heard. Imagine taking that part of your mind that judges what you say and turning if off and letting the words flow.

You can imagine yourself connecting with them and taking your knowledge of them from their very soul. After all, they are paying you for your reading.

The key is practice, practice, and more practice. I know one accomplished reader who would lay out a tarot spread for imaginary clients and give them readings.

Entertainment vs. Serious Reading

Let's make a distinction between cold readings done for entertainment and serious cold readings.

The easiest way to determine a serious cold reading is if someone is coming to you to help solve a problem or find direction in life. By contrast, a reading done for entertainment purposes are more lighthearted and easy. Many readings for entertainment are done at parties or corporate events, and it's unlikely that someone sitting with you is going enter or leave your session in tears. That cannot be promised with a serious reading.

Having done serious readings I can tell you that they are very taxing on the reader. A reader may be able to charge more for a serious sitting because they can be very demanding.

Becoming A Telephone Psychic

If you really want to do serious readings and don't know how to start then begin to look into the various "psychic phone networks" that are available. Before you do let me warn you. These psychic networks tend to charge the sitter $3+ a minute while the reader is getting about $12 per hour. The rest of money, over $180 per hour, is going into the pockets of the psychic network bureaucracy.

For some people working as a telephone psychic can be a very demanding but good experience. As a beginner it is one way to "cut your teeth" in doing readings.

What you'll find is that unless you are very good and can keep a caller on the line for more than 20 minutes you'll quickly lose your ranking in the psychic network. This means that you'll be shuffled to the very end of the line when they funnel callers your way. You'll likely have to be working very late night hours (that's when they advertise the most) before you get your ranking up again.

Corporate Readings

As for doing entertainment readings professionally, one way to get started is to introduce yourself to event planners and booking agents as "psychic entertainment," and make sure that you give them or their spouse a reading.

At these events you'll be given a table, or you can start by wandering around and introducing yourself as "psychic entertainment" and offer a palm or tarot reading.

Even if you are moderately good at cold reading you'll still be one of the most popular entertainers at these events.

Spontaneous Readings Just For Fun

Another way to do spontaneous psychic reading I learned from a friend who did it to meet women. He would simply go up to them extend his hand and say, "Hello, my name is Adrian. I just wanted to meet you." After the brief hand shake he would then turn their hand over and look at the palm intently, then smile at them and say, "Very nice. Thank you." Inevitably the woman would say "Wait, what did you see?" and he would explain he reads palms and he found her palm quite interesting. Very little else would need to be said as the every woman would insist to hear his reading.

Another way my friend Adrian would begin initiating a reading would be to say, "You have very interesting energy. Do you have a spiritual practice?" Regardless of the answer he would then say, "May I see your palm?" which would then initiate a very brief reading. He would then say, "This is probably boring you, I'll stop. Thank you." Usually the woman would say, "No, it's very interesting. Please go on," and so he would.

Another thing I learned from my friend Adrian was what I call an "unannounced reading." This would happen only when he felt confident that he could read something of the person that would shock them. He would then say it without warning. For example he might be talking with a very tall woman and say out of the blue, "I get this distinct impression that you've always felt embarrassed that you have big feet." The fact is most tall women have felt this in their lives, but it was he who "mysteriously" pulled that out of their mind.

Being able to do a psychic reading creates an opportunity for any reader to meet and speak with anyone who shows an interest. Simply by saying, "You have very nice energy. Do you have a spiritual practice?" can quickly lead to doing a psychic cold reading.

Another option is to attend a social engagement with a "wingman" whose job is to go around and tell people, "my friend is a psychic," to which you fain embarrassment and humility.

An Example Of a Spontaneous Psychic Reading

I had an interesting experience recently in being "psychic," and perhaps it can add to your influential power.

First, let me say that whenever I do a "psychic" experiment I'm always ready to be wrong, and it happens at times. What I've found is that people will completely forget the times you missed in a reading and over emphasize the times you got a "hit." It's just one of the well known facts of cold reading.

Okay, that said, here if what transpired.

I was speaking to a physical trainer about hypnosis and after some rapport building and resolving her curiosity about hypnosis I said, "could I do an experiment with you?"

Dantalion:	"Think of your birthday. Don't tell me, just think of it. Repeat it again and again in your mind. Is it 1987?"
Her:	"That's close. It's 1978." (The truth is I was guessing her age at 28 and I subtracted the dates wrong! Keep in mind for her it was still a hit!)
Dantalion:	I paused thinking..."Okay, you had birthday recently. Last month?"
Her:	"Yes".
Dantalion:	"Okay, the date will be harder. Is it the 28th?"
Her:	"No. It's the 13th. How did you do that?
Dantalion:	"Well, I practice with people, because you don't know until you test it and I'm willing to be wrong. For example, I'll go up to a store clerk and ask, "do you know someone named Marcia? (I paused) No, wait. It's Maria, isn't it? (I leaned forward and raised my eye brows)
Her:	"I do know someone named Maria. I've been thinking about her recently too."
Dantalion:	"...and she's married, isn't she?"
Her:	"Yes, she got married."
Dantalion:	"...and that was when you (I brought my hands

together and then separated them symbolizing a split).

Her: (Jaw dropping) "How did you know!" (Giving me a high five)

She explained how Maria's husband felt threatened with his new bride's single friends and forced the split.

Okay, a good portion of that was guessing and trusting my intuition, but keep in mind that I was wrong more than right.

So you ask, how did I do that? A deep understanding of cold reading skills, basic observation, and good guessing.

First, in spite of my bad math I assumed she was about 28. She still considered the reversed digits 87 and 78 "close."

How did I know she had a birthday last month? I didn't. It was a good guess. Had I missed it completely I would have stopped right there and it would have faded from her memory.

But I was right on the month. I had a one in twelve chance of getting it right and I used my best guess. So I pressed on to guess the date and missed. Before I guessed the date I prefaced it by saying, "this will be a lot harder," making any mistake more excusable. That was a good thing because I got it wrong.

My guessing her friend's name Maria was, in fact, about me talking to a store clerk. And I already know that female names beginning with M-A-R are very common. The girl also had a New York accent and looked Italian so a catholic name would get me even closer.

The realization of the split between her and Maria comes from my understanding of how many female relationships work out. First, the woman I was talking with seemed single – no ring on her hand. Most women her age and in her peer group will be married by that age. Also, it's very common that when new romances start (and marriages) old girl-girl relationships take a back seat and often fall to the wayside. I phrased that understanding (using my hand gestures) in such a way that she could fill in her own meaning.

Now, had any of my guessing been wrong then no problem. I shrug it off as if it was an interesting experiment.

So this is what it's like, and it's all done in good fun.

How To Be Good At Cold Reading

The Hook

It is **highly** recommended that as a psychic reader you have a story, what some people call a "hook" about how you gained your psychic abilities. It can be very mundane or very dramatic, but just be willing to tell it whenever someone asks.

A few examples of good hooks are...

"I learned to read cards and palms from my grandmother who brought her skills over from the old country. People in our neighborhood would visit her in these secret meetings where she would tell their fortunes. One day she sat me aside to teach me."

"I didn't know I was psychic until a psychic told me I was."

"Even when I was very young I could feel as if there was something beneath the surface of things, and when I started to tell people I got into a lot of trouble. Then it became clear that this was gift I have to use with some caution."

"There is nothing about me that I believe is psychic. It's when I start to talk to people and describe things about them that I had no way of knowing...then one begins to consider that something interesting is happening. Now I don't pretend to know what it is. All I know is that sometimes even I'm amazed at what I describe."

The Rules of Being a Good Cold Reader

Before going any further it is important to point out

22

that this attempt at describing psychic cold reading is not to discredit those people who truly feel they are psychic. This is merely a description of the psychic cold reading process.

What are the basic rules of cold reading?

1. Never refer to what you are doing as a "trick." This undermines the mysteriousness of what you are doing and can turn you into a trickster instead of someone that people want to learn from.

2. If you resort to some form of slight of hand or magic during the reading then under no circumstances reveal how it was done. These should be done rarely, if at all. If an amazed person asks how you do something (whether magic of psychic) it's best to be vague and quiet.

3. Practice. Practice as much as you can with as many people as possible. The more you practice the better you will get at reading people and being able to "talk on your feet" as if you were a psychic.

4. If you do use magic tricks during your psychic presentation use them sparingly and only to add impact to your presentation. Never do more than three or four unless you are getting paid for your psychic reading.

5. As much as possible avoid telling the sitter anything directly. Instead, you can use anything like the following statements: *"I feel..." "My intuition tells me ..." "The sense I get is that..." "The cards are telling me..." "There is an impression I'm getting ..."*

6.   Bill yourself as doing it only for entertainment while at the same time emphasizing that you have a serious intuitive gift.

7.   Some cold reading books would give you ethical reasons for never claiming to have supernatural powers. That does not forbid you from allowing people to think it. In fact, people will believe it more if they conclude it on their own without any explicit instructions. A few cold readers have made themselves more convincing by telling their sitter not to reveal that the psychic has an intuitive gift.

When starting any cold reading the one thing that will make all the difference is the belief that you can do a good cold reading. This belief helps make the process easy. I'm personally convinced that the one thing that prevents people from doing more cold readings is a lack of confidence. The solution is simply to believe that you can do good readings.

Ray Hyman's 13 Cold Reading Rules

1. Confidence is the key ingredient!

If you look and act as if you believe in what you are doing, you will be able to sell even a bad reading to most subjects. One danger of playing the role of reader is that you may actually begin to believe that you are really divining your subject's true character!

2. Use the latest statistical abstracts and polls.

These can provide you with much information about what various sub-classes in our society believe, do, want, worry about, etc. For example, if you can ascertain a subject's place of origin, educational level, and his or her parents' religion and vocations, you have gained information which should allow you to predict with high probability his or her voting preferences and attitudes to many subjects.

3. Set the stage for your reading.

Profess a modesty about your talents. Make no excessive claims so that you'll catch your subject off guard. You are not challenging them to a *battle of wits*. You can read the subject's character, whether he or she believes you or not.

4. Gain the subject's cooperation in advance.

Emphasize that the success of the reading depends as much on the subject's cooperation as on your efforts (after all, you imply, you already have a successful career at character reading. You're not on trial, your subject is!) State that due to difficulties of language and communication, you may not always convey the exact meaning you intend. In these cases, the subject must strive to *fit* the reading to his or her own life. You accomplish two valuable ends with this dodge. Firstly, you have an alibi in case the reading doesn't *click*; it's the subject's fault, not yours! Secondly, your subject will strive to fit your generalities to his or her specific life circumstances. Later, when the subject recalls the reading, you will be credited with much more detail than you actually provided! This is crucial. Your reading will only succeed to the degree that the subject is made an active participant in the reading. The good reader is the one who, deliberately or unwittingly, forces the subject to search his or her mind in order to make sense of your statements.

5. Use a gimmick.

The use of props serves two valuable purposes. Firstly, it lends *atmosphere* to the reading. Secondly, (and more importantly) it gives you time to formulate your next question or statement. Instead of just sitting there thinking of something to say, you can be *intently studying* the cards or crystal ball. You may opt to hold hands with your subject. This will help you feel the subject's reactions to your statements. If you are using, say, palmistry it will help if you have studied some manuals, and have learned the terminology. This will allow you to more quickly zero in on your subject's chief concerns - "do you wish to concentrate on the heart line or the wealth line?"

6. Have stock phrases at the tip of your tongue.

Even during a cold reading, a liberal sprinkling of stock phrases will add body to the reading and will help you fill in some time as you continue to formulate more precise characterizations. Use them to start your readings.

Astrology, palmistry, tarot and other fortune telling manuals are a key source of good phrases. Seriously, go to the book store and finger through a few of these books. When reading through them you'll find some really great phrases that you can add to your stock.

7. Keep your eyes open!

Use your other senses as well. Size the subject up by observing his or her clothes, jewelery, mannerisms and speech. Even a crude classification based on these can provide the basis for a good reading. Also, watch carefully for your subject's response to your statements - you will soon learn when you are hitting the mark!

An example of the value of being observant happened with a friend of mine who was doing a cold reading on a young lady. He peered down to notice the remnant of blue toe nail polish that revealed itself from her open toe shoes. "Your favorite color is blue." he stated in a matter of fact tone. Her jaw dropped.

8. Use the technique of fishing.

This is simply a device to get the subject to tell you about his or herself. Then you rephrase what you have been told and feed it back to the subject.

One way of fishing is to phrase each statement as a question, and then wait for the reply. If the reply or reaction is positive then you turn the statement into a positive assertion. Often the subject will respond by answering the implied question and then add more information. Later, the subject will forget that he or she was the source of the information! By turning your statements into questions you also force the subject to search his or her memory to retrieve specific instances to fit your general statement.

9. Learn to be a good listener.

During the course of a reading your client will be bursting to talk about incidents that are brought up. The good reader allows the client to talk at will. On one occasion I observed a tea leaf reader. The client actually spent 75% of the time talking. Afterward when I questioned the client about the reading and she vehemently insisted that she had not uttered a single word during the course of the reading. The client praised the reader for having astutely told her what in fact she herself had spoken.

Another value of close listening is that most clients that seek the services of a reader actually want someone to listen to their problems. In addition, many clients have already made up their minds about what choices they are going to make. They merely want support to carry out their decision.

10. Dramatize your reading.

This is so important. Give back what little information you do have or pick up a little bit at a time. Make it seem more than it is. Build word pictures around each divulgence. In the moment that you are speaking the words *believe and feel* what you are saying. Don't be afraid of hamming it up.

11. Give the impression you know more than you say.

The successful reader, like the family doctor, always acts as if he or she knows much more than they are letting on. Once you have persuaded the subject that you know one item of information that *you couldn't possibly have known* (through normal channels) the subject will assume that you know all! At this point the subject will open up and confide in you. You can do the following, but do it sparingly. Begin to speak about something that seems important but then, as if out of nowhere, stop...hesitate...change the subject, and then cautiously go back to it, choosing your words carefully as if you don't want to alarm the sitter with your information. It may sound something like this *"There is something that seems...pause)...well perhaps it's not quite as...(pause)...I'll get back to that in a moment."*

12. Flatter your subject at every opportunity.

An occasional subject will protest, but will still *lap it up*. In such cases, you can add, "you are always suspicious of those who flatter you. You just can't believe that someone will say something good about you without an ulterior motive."

13. The Golden Rule – Say what they want to hear!

The Structure of Cold Reading

If you are doing a complete reading for someone it's good to cover all the topics. The phrase to use as a mnemonic aide is "The Ides of March" or the letter I, M, A, R, C, H. These letters stand for the following:

Intelligence (and Emotion), **M**oney, **A**ppearance, **R**omance, **C**areer, **H**ealth

The paragraphs that follow are samples of what you can say on each of these topics. It's **HIGHLY** recommended that you memorize or create on your own a version of each of these paragraphs. The benefit in having these ready at hand is that they will give you a great start to follow up each topic. You'll also notice that your subjects will tend to be interested in one topic more that others.

As a general rule when you are saying these things you are supposed to be sensing impressions or "vibes," so it's a good idea to throw in "I sense," "I feel," "my intuition is telling me..."

Many people have a standard order in which they do these. If that works for you, great. Others cover these topics much more haphazardly. As you cover these topics they'll provide a great opportunity to give simple and common sense advise which will easily be accepted in a reading.

Intelligence and Emotion

"You have a very sharp mind. In fact, I sense that you perceive things and think about things on a slightly different level than most people. There are a few things that you will hold very close to the vest because you know some people aren't ready to know these things in the same way you are. You are one not inclined to put up with others nonsense. While you recognize the value of education in your life you value even more the education you've received from based on life experience."

Money

"I don't give investment advise, but I sense that in the area of money you are not a risk seeker. Unlike a lot of people I think you've come to the realization that money doesn't buy happiness, but it does solve a lot of problems. So first and foremost you've focused your money on problem solving and then on the fun that it can bring you."

Appearance

"As a child you were overly critical of yourself and your appearance, never being satisfied with your hair or your complexion; however, you began to gain more confidence as you grew older. I would say that you've learned a few things about how to deal with the opposite sex and you keep those secrets close to the vest and use them when you need to. A good perfume for you would be Obsession, Cartier, or Oscar de Laurenta.

Romance

(For women) "You've attracted plenty of the wrong type of men. But what you've learned is, of course, what you like. Any man you choose to show an interest in MUST have a sense of humor and has to be able to appreciate your off-beat sense of humor. You've learned a few things about how to attract men but you remain uncertain how to proceed when you meet someone who seems "out of your league." Nonetheless, your best instrument to attract men still remains your shy and flirtatious smile."

Career

"You are a person who is comfortable making decisions. You work easily in a management or supervisory capacity. I see someone who can set goals and move in a forthright manner to achieve them. You are not sick a lot and rarely miss work. One of your biggest professional desires is to be given to opportunity to prove what you know you're capable of. It would benefit you to not wait to be offered that chance, but instead, choose to act and genuinely prove your professional competence. This is where you must hold fast to your professional goals and ambitions."

Health

"You have to understand that I don't give medical advice so I can't advise on issues of illness. I can comment on health and the vitality of your body. There is a very good chance that you will outlive your spouse. Because you don't like taking pills or medications you seem to be healthier that others your age.

As an exercise use the "Ides of March" (Intelligence/Emotion, **M**oney, **A**ppearance, **R**omance, **C**areer, **H**ealth) as a format. Begin by writing, or better yet, speaking aloud qualities that fill each category. As you do this imagine connecting with your client and actually "reading" them during your non-stop monologue.

The Numerology System

The simplicity and ease of learning this system begins with a very basic knowledge of numerology.

To begin you will learn the readers "Soul Path Number," which will either be a single digit or the number 11 or 22.

To do this add together the day, month and year of their date of birth. So for example if someone is born on September 3rd 1978 you would add together. Thus 9 + 3 + 1978 = 1990 and then add together those numbers 1 + 9 + 9 + 0 = 19 and then adding those two digits together 1 + 9 =10 which will yield the final "Soul Path Number" of 1.

If at any point your total is either 11 or 22 don't reduce it any further and these are the numbers of "old souls" in numerology which will be explained.

Go ahead and determine what your soul path number is. Each of these numbers designate certain qualities within an individual and are referred to as "Soul Numbers."

Interpretations of the Soul Number

Soul Number 1

Mnemonic images: The Number one, The "I" as in "independence," and the word "Attainment."

More than anything else people with this number desire to be number one in all areas of their life. These often times flamboyant individuals crave being in the spotlight. They delight in experimentation and are the first to exploit a trend or new philosophy that will allow them to stand out from the crowd, hence the key word "independence." More than anything the almost childish one secretly desires unconditional approval from others they work with, and they work to achieve this by doing what they feel is the right thing in the eyes of others. They can be great successes in life and sometimes find that they are longing for the next project to work on. They may have a weakness of boasting about their deeds, which can help and hurt them in many ways. Their goal is to be enough in their own eyes to not have to boast.

Soul Number 2

Mnemonic images: The symbol of the yin/yang for duality. Keywords "cooperation," and "diplomacy."

Twos are often the power behind the throne, so to speak. They are able to smooth troubles and are appreciated for what they do. Individuals with this number have a deep desire to always be right, but they see things at a higher level and are able to move things and people in a diplomatic way.

As they often lead difficult lives that are fraught with criticism from others, especially in childhood, it is their desire for respect that leads them to be so difficult sometimes. They benefit most from developing an accepting and diplomatic approach when dealing with other people.

Soul Number 3

Mnemonic images: "self expression," and "creative."

Threes are creative and very good at starting things much more than finishing them. They are good talkers and can express themselves well. They don't like to work within restrictions but they learn, over time, that it's best when working with others to keep within the structures that are given them for success.

Threes have a great desire to be beautiful. In childhood they are usually the ugly ducklings, and even though many of them do grow into swans, they still often feel that there is something wrong with their appearance. They do not believe in aging gracefully, and many of them resort to plastic surgery in later years to defy the ravages of time. Some also become artists or photographers so that they can convey the importance of beauty to others.

Soul Number 4

Mnemonic images: "Hard work."

More than anything, fours crave emotional and financial security. As a result they will work very hard to achieve what they need first and then what they want second.

They can be clingy, possessive, and controlling of their loved ones. Their fear of taking risks can also cause them to be "stuck," especially when it comes to academics and career. They tend to stick to what they know works and react with hostility to any suggestion about change. Developing the confidence to handle anything that comes their way is the best way for fours to overcome their insecurity.

Soul Number 5

Mnemonic images: "freedom" and "variety."

Fives desire freedom more than anything else in their lives. They are somewhat claustrophobic and feel very confined by office jobs and routines. To avoid apathy and depression, fives should seek out careers that involve a great deal of travel, or a flexible time schedule. They function best as the owners of their own business or as entrepreneurs. Developing a regimen of spiritual study also greatly assists them as that helps them quell their restlessness and develop a sense of inner peace.

Soul Number 6

Mnemonic images: "home and family, responsibility."

Sixes ARE often taking responsibility far more than their fair share. They often find people, often family, giving them responsibilities they wouldn't otherwise take on. People who are a six often get involved in careers helping others.

They have a strong desire for justice at all costs. These proactive individuals consider themselves to be agents of karma, and often work behind the scenes to punish the undeserving and reward those who they consider to be underdogs. They are also perfectionists on many levels, and often make unrealistic demands on themselves and others in their never-ending quest to balance the score. To mitigate a tendency to resent all authority or judge a book by its cover, sixes need to learn tolerance and acceptance of others who do not share their opinions or moral standards.

Soul Number 7

Mnemonic images: seven heaven, the words "spirituality," "analysis," and "wisdom."

Number sevens find themselves on a different path than others. They are learners all the way through life and often end up with an affirming faith or philosophy that gives them strength. This differences make them a little bit harder to get close to, making it seem harder for them to fit in.

Sevens desire unconditional love. Many of them come from abusive or addicted families, so often they succumb to addiction or co-dependencies with toxic partners. They are often motivated by the urge to love others without conditions, as they have always desired the same for themselves. Unfortunately, their kindness is not always rewarded, as they tend to choose emotionally unavailable, mentally ill, or otherwise difficult partners. Individuals following this difficult soul path often learn several hard lessons about "letting go" of bad relationships before the end of their life.

Soul Number 8

Mnemonic images: "school," "social," and "generous."
Eights are practical creatures that value success above all else. Even as children many of them demonstrate an incredible ability to relate to other people, as well as make the right decisions regarding academics and career. Although they can appear selfish and materialistic to others, their actual desire (at least in the beginning) is to create a more prosperous future for their family, friends and community. Eights are usually generous and philanthropic individuals who don't feel that they deserve love unless they offer others a gift. Often they need to learn that aside from acquiring great wealth there are simpler routes to happiness.

Soul Number 9

Mnemonic images: "media," "flowers," and "funny."
Those born as a nine have a great desire to transcend all karma by using humor. Many are witty writers, public speakers and filmmakers. They are also great teachers, as they have a way of transforming spiritual messages and philosophies into entertainment for the masses. Most of them are gentle souls who have made it their life mission to make the world into a kinder place. Many of them are also liberal thinkers who support the right of each individual to make their own mistakes. Their motto is "remember to take time out to smell the flowers."

Soul Number 11

Mnemonic images: "eagle," "lemons to lemonade."

Eleven is a master soul number. The prime directive of these individuals is to transform the world through the use of spiritual knowledge, talents or tools. More than anything these individuals often desire to be as close to God or enlightenment as is possible in this world. Many have been born into bad situations that allow them to learn even more about the nature of life This eventually leads them to an incarnation as a "wounded healer" later in life that enables them to enlighten others.

Soul Number 22

Mnemonic images: "gardener," "transformer."

Twenty-twos are the master manifesters of the numerology divination system. These individuals rarely make a move in life without first making sure that their decisions are aligned with the guidance of something greater some might call it "divine will." These souls are sent to us to transform the world for the better. They accomplish this by combining practicality and genius with inspiration, intuition and a heartfelt desire to do what is best for all. Most of them believe that it is possible to build a Kingdom of Heaven on earth.

These are the beginnings of a very thorough cold reading system. Once you determine the sitter's soul number you can begin your reading with that information.

Doing psychic cold readings exercises a particular mental muscle that is capable of thinking on "a higher level."

To explain this, consider how the higher up the level of power you go the more you control. The same is true of knowledge. The more you know the more you can influence. Psychic readings require the reader to quickly observe someone and make global assumptions about them. The psychic reader gathers more information from their observation than the normal person, just by paying attention. From these observations the reader finds an artful way to describe what they've learned from their quick scan, and do it in such a way that the subject feels as if someone is reading their diary.

Being able to do a psychic reading creates an opportunity for any controller to meet and speak with anyone who shows an interest. The statement and question, "you have very nice energy. Do you have a spiritual practice?" can quickly lead to doing a psychic cold reading.

In a social or party setting people will quickly find a way to talk to the psychic in the room.

Before going any further it is important to point out that this attempt at describing psychic cold reading is not to discredit those people who truly feel they are psychic. This is merely a description of the psychic cold reading process.

The Astrology System

This section deals with an astrology system that can be integrated with the numerology system above.

First, I'd like to attribute a good portion of this section to Herb Dewey. Herb was one of the first to codify cold reading systems, and I encourage anyone interested in cold reading to read his work.

Below you'll learn very brief descriptions of the various personalities associated with the signs of the zodiac. There are only twelve, so with a bit of practice they will not be hard to remember. As you get further into the qualities of these astrological personalities you'll be able to add even more detail.

To start your reading you can mentally run through the zodiac signs and determine which best fits with the person you're reading. Without mentioning the sign begin to describe these qualities to the person. You can then ask which characteristics most closely describes themselves, and then ask for their birth sign.

Using this method you can apply it to any cold reading system including Tarot, numerology, auras, and others. Exercise your right brain and intuitive processes.

What follows is an abbreviated description of each of the zodiac personalities. Note that the dates roughly go from the 20th of the month to the 20th of the next month.

1. **Aries, the Ram** – March 21 – Pioneering, enthusiastic, courageous.

♈ Aries represents fiery self-will in action; pioneering energy; new growth seeking to emerge. The house where your Aries rules is where you will be challenged to grow and learn; where new things will keep emerging. Here you throw yourself into physical activity.

2. **Taurus, the Bull** – April 21 – Stable, Stubborn, well organized.

ŏ Taurus is deliberation and determination seeking practical productivity in this world. The house where Taurus rules is where you will be challenged to be practical and productive. Hang on to the things of this house for security.

3. **Gemini, the Twins** – May 21 – intellectual, adaptable, clever, often having two sides.

Ⅱ Gemini is abstract curiosity seeking to form a picture of the world, and to communicate those perceptions to others. The house where Gemini rules is where you will be challenged to learn by following your curiosity, and where communication will be important. It is also where you will be able to see both sides of an issue.

4. **Cancer, the Crab** – June 21 The Crab – sensitive, adaptable, clever.

♋ Cancer is healing, nurturing, sensitivity seeking psychological understanding, emotional self-expression, and the capacity to heal others. The house where Cancer rules is where you will be challenged to create a "safe place" in which to grow emotionally. Here you have deep feelings, and tend to be super-sensitive and defensive.

5. **Leo, the Lion** – July 21 – Bold, extroverted, generous, authoritative.

Leo is self-expression seeking confidence, ease, and honor in the social world. The house where your Leo rules is where you will be challenged to "shine," to apply the positive, creative qualities of your sun sign, and find a sense of inner peace.

6. **Virgo, the Virgin** – August 22 – critical, exacting, intelligent.

Virgo is analysis, refinement, and discrimination seeking perfection and purification of the self. This is the sign of the craftsman. The house where Virgo rules is where you will be challenged to analyze your feelings in a practical, unemotional way. Here is where you can serve others in a quiet, unassuming way.

7. **Libra, the Scales** – September 23 – harmonizing, just, sociable.

Libra is balance, harmony, and love of beauty seeking self-completion. The house where Libra rules is where you will be challenged to find balance. Here your ability to see both sides of any issue can lead to difficulty making choices.

8. **Scorpio, the Scorpion** – October 23 – secretive, strong, passionate.

Scorpio is intense emotional power probing and penetrating into the unconscious; seeking the power of transformation at work in ordinary reality; seeking to accept all that is frightening or overwhelming. The house where Scorpio rules is where you will be challenged to completely transform your life. You seek control in this part of your life and can be manipulative and secretive.

9. **Sagittarius, the Archer** – November 23 – honest, impulsive, optimistic.

Sagittarius represents an expansive quest to discover truth and the interconnectedness of all things. The house where Sagittarius rules is where you will be challenged to to expand your experiences. You are philosophical about the affairs of this house, and generous with its gifts.

10. **Capricorn, the Goat** – December 21 – ambitious, hard-working, cautious.

Capricorn is self-discipline and austerity seeking integrity and moral courage. The house where Capricorn rules is where you will be challenged to win respect and recognition from others. You tend to combine traditional and original approaches to the affairs of this house, or feel the frustration of being torn between the two.

11. Aquarius, the Water Bearer – January 20 – original open-minded, independent.

Aquarius is eccentricity and radical individuality seeking freedom of the soul and communication with the group mind. The house where Aquarius rules is where you will be challenged to seek new knowledge in order to break down old ideas. Here you are very much ahead of your time.

12. **Pisces, the Fish** – February 19 – kind, sensitive, creative.

)(Pisces is mystical dreaminess, warmth, and healing compassion seeking self-transcendence. The house where Pisces rules is where you will be challenged to discern between illumination and illusion. Here is a doorway, either to higher spiritual knowledge or to escape through day-dreaming or self-indulgence. It's difficult to learn to trust and follow your intuition, and you will feel as if you are acting blindly.

There is a simple way to begin a cold reading based on the astrological system. You start by simply guessing which astrological sign bests fits your reader and begin to describe the qualities of that sign without mentioning the sign itself.

After giving an initial "impression" a friend of mine would ask the reader, "tell me, what is your favorite time of year?" What he found is that on average people's favorite time of year is most often the same season as the month in which they were born (of course this is not fail safe but simply a generalization). So, typically when someone says "winter" it is a good guess that they were born around December or January. He would then add the qualities of a zodiac sign of that season and then as a throw away comment say something like "that is typical of a (name of sign)."

If he is wrong no one comments because it was a statement said in passing. After all he didn't say, "you're a (name of sign)." But if he is right he will be hailed with praise and recognition for his psychic ability.

Notice that on the book cover is an illustration of the circle of the zodiac. It can be seen as if it were a clock face with each sign of the zodiac at the location of a number on the clock. This image is what Herb Dewey, famous psychic cold reader, referred to as "The Telltale Clock."

If you lay the book down nearby it can make a useful crib sheet while doing a reading, and no one will be the wiser.

Note that each sign is located in a position where a clock number is located. One o'clock is Aries, Two o'clock is Taurus, Three o'clock is Gemini, and so on. You now have their lucky number which is their number on the clock.

Cold Reading Tips and Tricks

So what does a non-psychic cold reader use to give people a good and entertaining psychic reading?

The first tool is sensory acuity and being a good observer. With experience and a bit of study anyone can learn how to read someone based on their age, dress, posture, jewelery, hair style, and how they interact with people. Based on this information the reader makes opening statements and intersperses them with statements that are likely to be true.

What you'll find when you talk to other cold readers is that they discover and collect their own set of clues and scripts. Some of these clues include:

Right/Left Handedness: People who wear their watch on the right wrist are likely left handed. The reader can say:

"You grew up knowing that something was different and you tried hard to fit in. You notice how a lot of people are conformists and how you are different."

Red Heads: Red headed people, especially with curly hair and freckles, will find the following statement generally true.

"I can tell that for you there was some trouble you had with people seeing you as being different. You even got a bit of teasing when you were younger. Eventually what you found is that you had to find a balance between being different to meet their expectations and deciding that what they thought was not your concern."

Professional Drivers: Cab drivers and truck drivers will almost consistently complain of lower back pain.

Jewelry: People, especially women, who wear a lot of jewelry (and make-up), will very likely find the following statement true for them.

"You try to hide your concern about how people perceive you. You want to always create a positive first impression because you know how important it is, and it will allow you to more easily reveal that part of you this is deeper...the part of you that has more depth and is not so easily seen at first glance."

Eye Movement: During a reading people may be rapt by what you say with eyes locked on you, or their eyes will be darting back and forth trying to find out internally if your statements are true for them. In this latter case, and with people who are more skeptical, the following statement can be used.

"You don't always take things at face value. You make a point of testing out what people tell you as fact."

Attractive Women: Very attractive women will often find the following statements true.

"You have a habit of attracting the wrong type of man," and *"even though you are often told that you are attractive you find that you are your own worst critic, never truly satisfied with what you have and always looking for some area that might need improvement."*

The Scar: Most people will have a scar on their left knee. Don't ask me why. I don't know. If you say the following script and the scar is actually on the right knee you can recover simply by saying "oh yes, that's my left and your right."

"I see that as a child you were very active and you worried your parents and...you have a scar on your left knee."

The Triangle: I love this one. It works great whenever you are working with an exotic dancer. It implies that someone is in the midst of a lovers triangle but it can easily apply to many other interpretations.

"I'm sensing a pull of energies. Something like a triangle with you being one of it's points being effected or pulled by the other points of the triangle. It seems as if there are some decisions you are putting off."

Your Client's Background: Consider the background of your client. When you recognize someone who is likely to of Irish Catholic background it's a strong likelihood they know someone named Mary or Patrick. They may very well likely be from a larger family.

Magical Metaphors

Practice thinking and speaking in metaphors. This can be a fun game to play and when done well people love it. A metaphor is story that has some relationship to the client's experience. This could be a story about a "little girl" or a "man on a quest" or a "man in search of peace of mind," but at no time do you say the story is about the client. This leaves it up to the client to determine who the story is about.

When telling a story about a *"man on a quest who is trying to complete some unfinished business,"* you'll find that it could be about the client or a moment in the clients past. It could be about their brother or uncle or even a dead relative speaking from beyond the grave. Let them tell you who it is about.

Speaking in metaphors is very powerful because the client determines who it is about. Be prepared because people often respond to a good metaphor or story with very strong emotions.

Frustration

It's worth remembering that as a general rule the reason people visit psychiatrists and psychics is a strong feeling of frustration for not having been able to attain ideals, fullfill ambitions, realize goals, and get ahead in their work. Knowing this can simple be stated and most people will agree.

"There is a frustration. A part of this reading has to do with a level of desire that has resulted in frustration. Ambitions, goals, plans that you want to fulfill have been driving you… yet they have not been fully fulfilled." This is where you can offer encouragement. *"It will be wise for you to know that as long as you hold to your goal you can think of it as inevitable. If your goals are important to you then you should hold to it and continue to uncover progress towards your goal."*

Personal Magnetism

As a psychic reader you can't lose when you mention your client's ability to influence others. This is true regardless of whether they are attractive or plain, outgoing or introverted. If your subject is seems shy or introverted it is a good idea to offer encouragement to exercise their latent charm.

"Your personal magnetism is quite strong, and has been a

big factor in overcoming many adverse influences. But you may notice a tendency to let it remain dormant and unexploited. You do possess a power to charm and fascinate others with whom you come in contact, yet you are most susceptible to the influence of others – and not always for your own good."

Procrastination

Procrastination is an area that almost all people will agree is a problem for themselves. This fact gives you two opportunities: the opportunity to amaze the client, and to give them encouragement for improvement.

"One of your weaknesses is putting things off that you should get done. This is a weakness you should try to correct. After all, procrastination is the thief of time. It is due to this tendency that you find yourself rushing around and never having enough time for yourself. This makes you anxious and uptight, and then you cannot relax. You know what is important in your life and you need to use that to motivate yourself into action. When you step back and look at your life you will find that you've accomplished the most when you focus in on what you're most passionate about. Agreed?"

Shoes News

According to Herb Dewey you can gain loads of information about a person my looking at their shoes. Notice how the shoes are coordinated with the outfit color and style, cost, and whether or not they are cared for. Does he have white socks with black leather shoes? Are they work type shoes, as with nurses and mechanics, or western boots? Do the shoes match a belt or hand bag.

Ideas Within The Clients Name

If the reader is ever stuck for ideas consider that there is nothing more important that the person's name. The name can be wonderful resource by using the letters as a mnemonic. If the person's name is Fiona the reader can use F-I-O-N-A as a tool.

F – might stand for faith, fair, feminine, forgiving, far-sighted

I – idealistic, imaginative, independent, intuitive

O – open, orderly, outdoors, out grown.

N – new, neat, natural

A – accepting, ambitious, able, assertive

By using the client's name in this manner the reader can apply these qualities to any predicted challenge or obstacle.

"If I'm in error..."

Freely say through out your reading these words:

"If at any time I'm in error, please advise me."

This will let the client know that you are open to good direction and not cocky and infallible.

The Forer Effect

As an exercise begin to make a list of the following statements and concepts, add your own, and first and foremost practice, practice, practice.

Generalized statements that most people agree with.

The Forer Effect is a psychological phenomenon described in 1949 by Bertam Forer. The Forer Effect occurs when a very general statements are said to someone in order to describe their personality, and the person most often agrees that it is true, remembering the statements that are favorable and accurate and dismissing and forgetting those statements that are inaccurate. This selectivity of the human mind allows the person receiving the psychic reading to retrofit the information in order to accept it as true.

For example, Forer gave a personality test to people and **each person was given the same personality description below**. Most people agreed that it was an accurate description of their personality.

"Some of your aspirations tend to be pretty unrealistic. At times you are extroverted, affable, sociable while at other times you are introverted and reserved. You have found it unwise to be too frank in revealing yourself to others. You pride yourself on being an independent thinker and do not accept others opinions without satisfactory proof. You prefer a certain amount of change and variety, and you become dissatisfied when hemmed in by restrictions and limitations. At times you have serious doubts as to whether you have made the right decision or done the right thing. Disciplined and controlled on the

outside, you tend to be worrisome and insecure on the inside."

"Your sexual adjustment has presented some problems for you. While you have some personality weaknesses, you are generally able to compensate for them. You have a great deal of unused capacity which you have not turned to your advantage. You have a tendency to be critical of yourself. You have a strong need for other people to like you and for them to admire you."

"People close to you have been taking advantage of you. Your basic honesty has been getting in your way. Many opportunities that you have had offered to you in the past have had to be surrendered because you refuse to take advantage of others. You like to read books and articles to improve your mind. In fact, if you are not already in some sort of personal service business, you should be. You have an infinite capacity for understanding people's problems and you can sympathize with them. But you are firm when confronted with obstinacy or outright stupidity. Law enforcement would be another field you understand. Your sense of justice is quite strong."

"You often try to leave an impression on your surroundings that you are stern and rigid, while you are actually an emotional and vulnerable person. Sometimes you are bright, communicative and social, but you can turn into yourself, and in those times it is hard for people around you to reach your thoughts. You like changes and are dynamic, and lack of freedom can make you discontent, even melancholic and depressive. You know that you are a person that has an attitude and you don't take random opinions without hard evidence. You have an amazing ability to understand people who surround you and who you love. You also have a well-developed sense for rightfulness, and it is hardest for you to accept human greed and a lack

of feeling for others."

"In your love life you had lesser problems. Still, aside for a few weaknesses, your inner strength provided you with the means to successfully diminish them. You are often expressing criticism about yourself, even more than it is necessary. The main cause is that you have a strong need to be accepted and loved, and you turn too strict when it comes to your character."

"You are aware that you hold significant potential that you still haven't completely put to work because of your reticence and insecurity. Soon you will learn how to put your abilities to full use."

A very useful type of statement to you that is part of the Forer effect is what I call the "half and half." The half and half is saying that you have quality X, but you also demonstrate times where you have it's opposite. You can't lose with this one.

"You tend to be outgoing and upbeat but there are times that you need to conserve your energies and spend time with yourself."

Doing this is not hard. Start with your impression of what might be true for the individual you are reading and then conclude the half-and-half statement with *"but there are times when..."* and mention it's opposite.

Ian Rowland's Elements of a Reading

One the best books on cold reading that I can recommend is "The Full Fact Book of Cold Reading" by Ian Rowland. It is not on amazon.com but can be found on the Internet with a little effort.

With his book Ian Rowland offers details into what he calls "the elements of a cold reading." For the sake of brevity and so as not to infringe on his work I've offered a synopsis and paraphrase of these wonderful elements. I fully encourage you to seek out his book to study these concept more in depth.

Elements concerning facts and events in a reading

1) The Rainbow Ruse: This is a statement that credits the client with both a certain quality *and* its opposite. For example:

"You have a very strong personality that will stand up to people when confronted. On the other hand you can easily look back and remember times that you wish you had been more resolute and faced certain people and situations head on."

2) Fine Flattery: This is a statement that is designed to flatter the client in a way likely to win agreement. Something like *"you are wonderfully hard working,"* or my favorite, *"you're a real flirt!"*

3) The Psychic Credit: A psychic credit tells the client that they have some latent form of psychic ability or unrecognized divine power. A psychic once told me "you are an ascended master."

4) Sugar Lumps: The sugar lump relates to the client's willingness to be open to the idea of psychic phenomena, and it used as a reward for accepting the reading.

"You have your own very strong sense of intuition, and this is why this type of reading can work especially well for you."

5) The Jacques Statement: These are statements that reflect the various stages we go through in life. These stages include times like adolescence, rites of passage (anything like first job, first kiss, first relationship) and crises that are common to people (lost love, job, death of loved one, dropping out of school). Jacques statements are often vague enough for the client to put their own meaning to them.

"You have found yourself wondering about what happened to your hopes and dreams."

"You have a definite strategy for your career, but you'll find that there have been more unforeseen things in your path than you could have predicted."

6) Greener Grass: A "Greener Grass" element focuses on the an option that the reader did **not** take. This is something that we all find ourselves pondering at time yet seldom speak about. For example:

"you are very focused and try to firmly keep your hand upon the wheel; nonetheless, you find yourself wondering about certain options in your career and especially in your relationships that you thought weren't best for you at the time."

7) Barnum Statements: Barnum statements describe aspects of the client that would, in fact, apply correctly to most people. Examples include:

"You tend to feel you have a lot of under utilized ability."

"When you are bothered by someone you make a point of holding your tongue and give them the first opportunity to set things right."

"When considering your mistakes you give yourself a harder time than anybody. You are your own best, or worst, critic."

8) Fuzzy Fact: A Fuzzy Fact is something that is stated as factual and contains two qualities. First, it is very likely to be accepted as fact and secondly, it is general enough that it leaves room to be developed into something more specific.

"I see a very meaningful event that happened close to a birthday or holiday."

"Job or career transition is going to be considered."

9) The Good Chance Guess: This is a guess that has a better than average chance of being correct.

"You were quite active as a child and people were concerned about your well being. However, in spite of this you have a scar on your left knee."

By the way, you would be surprised how accurate that guess is! Maybe you have one yourself.

10) The Lucky Guess: A lucky guess is sometime nothing more than a name, location or date that the psychic is guessing has some meaning for the client. There is no subtlety to a lucky guess. It's just what is says, a guess without strategy behind it.

"There is a name, Robert, Bob or Rob that has some meaning for you."

11) The Stat Fact: A Stat Fact is a statement that is based on statistical information and demographics. This is where the Internet, a library or a commercial database come in *very* handy.

12) The Trivia Stat: Different from a stat fact, a trivia stat is personal and relatively insignificant. Ian Rowland offers these that he has collected over the years:

- *There is a box of old unsorted photographs that you would like to go through.*

- *You have expired medicine in your bathroom.*

- *You have a single earring as the partner to it is missing.*

- *You've had problems with your car - left rear wheel or tire.*

13) The Cultural Trend: Cultural trends can be used in a psychic reading by simply being aware of what is happening in popular culture.

14) The Childhood Memory: As the name implies, this is the simple description of something that happens as a child.

"I'm getting the impression that when you were young you

had a particular interest that you devoted a great deal of your time to. This reading is indicating something that is artistic or perhaps athletic."

15) Folk Wisdom: *The is where you need to study up on your folksy cliches.*

"Two heads really are better than one."

"There's quite definitely light at the end of the tunnel."

"Don't let the idea of skeletons in your closet slow you down."

16) The Seasonal Touch: Here the psychic offers statements based on the time of year or other seasonal factors. These obviously vary according to the country, culture and society in which the psychic is giving the reading. Nearing Christmas the psychic might say...

"You find yourself pondering decisions regarding friends and relatives and how to best interact with them."

17) The Opposites Game: The Opposites Game is a very wise strategy, and by "wise" I mean sneaky. The psychic first suggests to the client that there is someone in her life whom she does not get along with, or with whom she feels friction. The psychic then describes this "awkward" or "unhelpful" person in some detail.

To do this, the psychic simply endeavors to describe someone who would be the exact opposite of the client!

For example, if the client is fun and lighthearted and you describe the opposite as serious and stern it's more than likely the client knows someone who fits the description.

18) The Push Statement: A Push Statement is difficult to describe but can be very powerful when done well. While most to these element are designed to get a "hit" the push statement is designed to elicit a "miss" from the client...at least at first. If the psychic delivers it with confidence and then expands the context it can usually be made to fit. The result is the client agrees and says "oh, yeah! I do know what you're talking about now!"

According to Ian Rowland, Push statements are hard to make up and will tend to evolve over many readings and should be used sparingly. The key is to give enough elements that eventually *something* begins to fit for the client.

Elements concerning extracting information

19) The Direct Question: Obviously, this is the simplest way to getting information. It should be noted that some readings can be FILLED with direct questions, but it's best to not go overboard.

"What is on your mind?" is a direct question that will cause little suspicion. You can be a bit more sneaky with your direct questions.

"A reading can go anyway you want. From experience there are things that often weigh on peoples' minds...things they want to know about before they have a reading. You may have given some thought to this already. So that no time is wasted, what direction would you like to focus on to start this reading?"

A very tricky way of hiding a direct question has to do with a combination of tonality and gesture. Typically the tonality of a question (in English) goes up. Also there is an unconscious gesture many people do of raising the eyebrows and nodding the head slightly while asking a question. This tends to signal that "this is a question."

The trick is to make the question tonality go down, as if giving an order, and while doing the unconscious head gesture. Then pausing long enough for the client to fill the silence.

So, instead of asking "is there a problem in your relationship?" you make it sound like the statement, "your relationship problems," and with the questioning eyebrow raise and head nod.

20) The Incidental Question: The incidental question takes the form of chatty conversation.

"...now why would that be?"

"...is this making sense to you?"

"...can you relate to this?"

"...does this sound right?"

"...would you say this is along the right lines for you?"

"...this is significant to you, isn't it?"

"...you can connect with this can't you?"

These can be slipped in as you reveal things using the other 38 elements of cold reading.

21) The Veiled Question: The veiled question is a statement that is followed by an incidental question.

"I'm getting the impression...not clear really...still...an impression...that there are three forces, energies perhaps, people vying for position...and this impression is that you are one of the three. Does this make sense to you?"

The "three forces" monologue is a great way to extract romantic triangles from someone. The incidental question can be hidden further by explaining that you don't know if this is something that is happening now or in the past. This will widen the net even further for the client to find a working explanation.

22) The Diverted Question: The diverted question takes a piece of solid information and extrapolates unspoken details that are very likely to be correct. The solid piece of information could come from a direct question, or noticing the type of car the client drives or any friends they might be with. Some psychics are well versed in how an expensive purse is different from a look-alike knock off purse. This says volumes for the reading.

"I see that you have a keen eye. First your eye is always set toward quality. You know what a good name brand is worth, but your eye is also very shrewd to finding the best deal."

23) The Jargon Blitz: This can often be described as the "baffle them with bullshit" tactic. It does two things. First it establishes you as an authority in your method of reading (astrology, tarot, palmistry) by spewing out terms of your field most people have not put in the time to learn. Secondly, as you use these terms to describe the reading the client will put whatever meaning to it that best fits.

"The two of swords is a card of the mind. In fact, it

means that there is a decision that is being weighed. The five of wands goes well with this as it indicates there is a struggle...not a major one...but a bothersome one. These are conjoined cards which means that the struggle is affecting this decision. I don't know if this makes sense to you."

You are welcome to throw in completely unrelated jargon like "form a divergence" or "conjoined cards"

24) The Vanishing Negative: The vanishing negative is tricky and cute. You ask a question in the negative and whatever the response is you say, "ah, I thought so."

"You don't have a cat do you?"
"No, no pets."
"Yes, I thought so."

"You don't have a cat do you?"
"Not now but I did."
"Yes, I see you having quite an affinity toward felines and that cat meant a lot to you."

The steps that follow a vanishing negative are **Affirm, Reassure, and Expand**. So after you deliver the "I thought so..." go into some small detail as in the example above, and then expand.

"You are going to have a cat of one sort or another throughout your life. In fact, you'll discover that the ones you keep you never have to look for. They find you and that is how you'll know it's right."

25) The Sherlock Strategy: The Sherlock strategy is about being a good deductive detective. The psychic observes the client and makes deductions from what they see.

If the client is wearing their watch on their right arm it is more likely they are left handed. From that the psychic can say:

"Growing up you immediately knew you were different. Some people tried hard to make you fit into their way of the world but you held firm. You had some trouble early in life trying to match up to how other people learned but you quickly began to excel."

Knowing how guitar players get callouses on the tips of their fingers can be used a lot of different ways.

"The Hanged Man card indicates that you possess a strong creative instinct that you try very hard to express. My intuition is saying that it's music and that you sing too. You consider yourself a better musician than a vocalist, but I want to remind you you should never be discouraged."

26) The Russian Doll: The Russian Doll is a way of "peeling the onion" so to speak, when a statement doesn't give you hit.

"I'm getting the impression of that you're making a move right now. Does that make sense?"
"No."
"Oh this could be not you per say, but someone close to you."
"No."
"Oh, not so much a physical move but really a transition...a major change of sorts."
"Well, my brother-in-law is finally getting a job."
"That's why this sticks out in my mind so much. This is long overdue!"

It took three attempts to get a hit and the misses fall by the wayside. The key to the Russian Doll is if something doesn't match up then expand it into a different context.

Elements concerning future predictions

27) Peter Pan Prediction: The Peter Pan Prediction tells the client what they want most to hear. This should not be underestimated as it validates the reason people get psychic readings in the first place. Generally this will include the areas of health, relationships and finance.

28) Pollyanna Pearls: The simple formula for a Pollyanna Pearl is to give a positive prediction in a specific area that the client has been having trouble.

"According to your chart there is an indication that in the last six to twelve months there has been some financial concerns that have weighed heavily on your mind. But as you progress over the next ten weeks this will lighten."

"You are a worrier, especially when it comes to your relationships. There have been some struggles for you. It's been a challenge at times, but the cards are indicating a very sharp turnaround! My goodness! There is definitely something in store for you in the area of romance."

Remember that everyone likes to hear good news, and because these are not verifiable predictions you can't go wrong.

29) Certain Predictions: Why not make predictions that simply can't go wrong? That is the power of a certain prediction. All you have to do is leave out *when* it's going to happen.

"You're going to run into a bit of financial stress, but you'll find, looking back, you dealt with it quite well."

"A new person is going to enter your life."

30) 50/50 Predictions: These are predictions that can only go one of two ways. Win or lose. Pass or fail. Act or do nothing. Get it or don't get it. With the odds being a flat 50/50 the key is to deliver your answer with unshakable confidence. When you're right you take the credit. If there is a miss then who is going to call it to your attention? Likely no one.

One way to overcome that possibility is to preface your reading with a caveat:

"While I'm absolutely certain of what I predict this isn't to say that you cannot intervene in your destiny. In fact, you can. What I will tell you are not unchangeable certainties but merely tendencies that are in place right now. The good news is that you are the person in control of your life. Do we agree?"

"Am I always right? No, of course not. There are a few times I've only come close to my predictions but more often you'll find I'm right with what I've said would happen."

31) Likely Predictions: Of course a likely prediction stands a reasonable chance of taking place, and is different from a certain prediction in that the time line for the prediction is given.

"There is someone you haven't heard from in a while that is going to contact you this next month."

"Within the next year there will be an accident involving you...or a family member...nothing major. Mostly cuts and scrapes."

32) Unlikely Predictions: A good unlikely prediction will also give a psychic some credibility. Who else would be willing to go out on a limb to confidently predict something so unlikely?

"In the next month you're going to find someone who shares your birthday. This is going to prove a very supportive friendship."

"I need to put you at ease here. In the next month a mirror is going to break and you can relax. There is no seven years of bad luck. Got it? So put that out of your mind. Shrug it off and let it go."

Unlikely predictions have value in that the few that come true carry HUGE press potential that can be used to further the psychic's credibility and exposure. One successful unlikely prediction is like a prize cow that should be milked for all it's worth.

33) Factual Predictions: This is a blind guess about something in the medium future.

"You're going to have a vacation in March."

34) Self-fulfilling Predictions: There is a story of a poor man who went to a psychic to be told that he was Napoleon in a past life and is obligated to live up to the stature of his former life. He went on to overcome his challenges and feeble surroundings only to discover much later that the psychic was a fraud. But it was too late. He had already proven that he had Napoleonic strengths and he could not go back.

Let that be your goal when you offer a self-fulfilling prediction.

"There are going to be a few challenges for you, but soon you'll begin to recognize that challenges are there to be overcome. You'll take on a more positive attitude toward life and agree to face life head-on. It will take some work...and you'll work hard at it...to realize that nothing can upset you unless you let it."

If you consider yourself a good judge of people it's good to let the positive self-fulfilling prediction fit the client. The list of positive self-fulfilling predictions are many:

- *Resolve a relationship problem*

- *Make new friends*

- *Become more sociable*

- *Let go of old grudges*

- *Refocus on faded goals*

- *Renew determination*

- *Make a fresh start*

- *Turn over a new leaf*

35) Vague Predictions: Vagueness in psychic predictions

can be considered high art.

"There is a transition that is taking place."

"I see a new source of satisfaction in your life."

      I would like to note that if one wants to read a huge volume of vague descriptions and predictions that they purchase a kit called "The Astrology Kit" and read the book in it called "The Horoscope Reading." Any page in it will do.

36) Unverifiable Predictions: One reason people come to psychics is to get information that they can't confirm or uncover. This lends a certain ease to telling a client something they have no way of being able to confirm or deny.

"Someone is holding a grudge against you and working to sabotage you. What they don't know is how your very nature will defeat whatever they attempt. You won't even have to think about it. That is your strength"

"At your place of work there are some back door dealings that others are working on. They initially hope to include you only to realize they must fall back onto their original plans."

37) One-way Verifiable Predictions: A one-way verifiable prediction is one that can be verified only if it comes true.

"You're going to be offered one of several business opportunities, but the time won't be right for you and you'll decide against it."

"A friend will call you that you haven't heard from in a long

time. They will have wanted to call you for a while but were putting it off."

38) The Never-was Prediction: The never-was prediction is not a cold reading technique but a public relations tool to be used to impress the people and the media if they are being interviewed.

To do a never-was prediction the psychic only *says* they predicted something that came true. Make sure to build a nice but unverifiable story around it and to mention it only in passing.

The truth is that the prediction was NEVER made. It's what the rest of us call a lie.

Stock Lines for Cold Reading

Stock lines help elicit the Forer Effect in that these are lines that can be generally accepted as true by most people.

It's a good idea to read through these lines and find ways to intersperse them in your reading. It's a good idea to try to "read" your subject to your best ability to make sure the line fits them.

You're getting a lot of good stock lines. Hopefully after you read enough of these lines you'll see that it's not too hard to start making up some stock lines of your own. That will be a demonstration of your genius.

"There is a certain ambition that you have that you tend to keep very personal. Perhaps your closet friends have sensed it."

"I sense you have some very strong values with regards to family, and you're often willing to put the needs of others above your own. This is especially true with those people whom you are closest to. In this way you are loyal and honest. At times you feel that your kindness to others is not always returned. I sense that this troubles you somewhat, but you should not let it. These people do care about you just as deeply; however they sometimes have difficulty showing it."

"You ability to communicate is quite strong. You stand above those around you in that respect. In may ways you have the ability of a natural leader. You are very bright and capable but most importantly someone who can see beneath the surface of things. Others find you fun to be around."

"My sense is also that people in your personal life and at work look at you as a problem solver. This means that you're able to find a happy medium when in a tight spot."

"Whatever happens to you, good or bad, your life is never going to be dull. Between your aggressiveness and vitality, your conviction of your own worth, and the way you are able to make the world believe in it, you will have your ups and downs."

"You like to know that you're acknowledged and receive some recognition, but for it's own sake rather than for wealth."

"Disappointment in some early love matters warps your emotional nature and is likely to effect the way you think about relationships."

"You have an inner drive of ambition that leads to almost inevitably to success. You're a hard person to manipulate even though you do give people a lot of leeway and are willing to compromise a lot."

"Your life has the potential of developing very rapidly when you set your mind to some intention. This is especially true for you when you are at your most passionate. That ability demonstrates the potential of your ability to lead."

"You are capable of envisioning great schemes, plans, and ventures, and of putting them across."

(For the person who appears physically fit) *"Your animal nature is strong. You have a strong vigorous energy and a temperament that is shot through with vitality which can burst forth as either anger or a seething passion. On the one hand you want control, but you don't want to appear controlling and you're probably well aware of this duality. Some people may say that your daring takes the world by storm."*

"You know when to stand and fight and when to run and protect your assets."

"You are not truly as self-confident as you impress the world with, for what you aspire to demands a very strong presentation - one strong enough to camouflage any of your own personal doubts. This leaves you in a position to more thoroughly analyze your internal state of mind without it effecting what you are going after."

"Mental power is your strength – and your weakness. It is your strength because you are rational and able to work things our analytically seeing the details of things. It is your weakness because if you get too absorbed in mental matters you can tend to overlook your emotional well being."

"You possess a duality. On the one hand you can be very reserved and thoughtful. On the other hand there are times when you can cut loose and put aside the roles that other people see you in."

Except for the fact that many people wanting a reading also want to hear more than just about their personality it is possible to give the very same basic reading by simply having a script that includes these types of statements.

The following is a list of the most common topics that people are interested in during a psychic reading. It would be a good idea to write a list of responses to each of these topics that will apply to most people and give good general recommendations.

I did pick up some great lines listening to online psychic radio. Here's one that can be said to older middle-aged women:

"How's that book you're writing coming along?"

It's a great line since many women from that age bracket are at least thinking about writing a book, if not having started already.

"In the year ahead, you could become involved in several challenging new projects that are loaded with great possibilities."

"An important objective can be achieved today and will be far easier than you anticipated, but it might not come about in the manner that you like."

"Abundant opportunities will be at your disposal in the year ahead."

"Many of the restrictions that hampered you in the past will be alleviated in the year ahead."

"New projects?" "Great possibilities?" "An important objective?" "Abundant opportunities?" "The restrictions?" Which ones? Financial, romantic, business, personal, professional? And what about "involved in," "at your disposal," and "will be alleviated?" What exactly do these phrases mean?

Giving covert suggestions during a psychic reading

A psychic reading is a great place to give embedded commands and other hypnotic types of like. For example, it is nice to have someone who is responsive to the psychic's reading and is paying attention, so the reader can make those commands a part of the reading.

*"You seem like someone who can really...**focus in**...on something when it is right in front of you...and you...**find it interesting**...there are certain things that do **get your attention**. One of those things is when you have a chance to **learn about yourself**..."*

Understanding personality types

A little psychology can go a LONG ways when doing psychic cold readings. Take personality types for example.

There are plenty of great resources online and in books to help anyone learn about personality types and use them in cold readings. The description here is just enough to get you headed in the right direction.

There are many different ways of categorizing personalities and any of them will be useful for you. The most common is the Meyers-Briggs Type Indicator that consists of four personality qualities that each have two possible choices.

Social Orientation: Extrovert (E) or Introverted (I)
Information Gathering: Sensation (S) or Intuition (N)
Decision Process: Thinking (T) or Feeling (F)
Relationship to World: Judgment (J) or Perception(P)

By understanding variations of personality a reading can quickly conclude things about people from a very brief observation which can add huge amount of content to the reading. For example, if someone appears reserved and introverted the following statement will be easy for them to accept as true

"Time with yourself is very important. Even though you have people in your life you interact with you are most comfortable dealing with your own thoughts and feelings."

An extroverted personality would easily accept this statement as true:

"You have a great ability to enjoy the company of others. Sure, there are times when you need to collect your thoughts and be alone, but you can easily devote your time to others and be energized by those interactions."

Tarot cards and palmistry

Tarot cards and palmistry can be a great resource for a cold reader because they naturally give the impression of authority. When people see you doing a tarot card reading they are going to instantly assume you've put in the time to learn this mysterious craft and know what you are talking about. Another benefit is that people tend to lose their inhibitions and openly ask for a tarot card or palm reading when they see it done to others in a social setting.

Tarot cards and palmistry are skills that require a certain amount of practice, but the benefit in learning these skills is that the reader gives credit to the system instead of themselves. In other words, anything in the reading that is inaccurate or unfavorable are simply attributed to *"what the cards say."*

Tricks of guile – Mentalism

Mentalism is a field of magic that appears to be mind reading when in fact it is simple magic and trickery. Doing a search online or in a book store will give a wealth of resources to incorporate a few mentalism tricks into your cold reading routine.

Here is one of the simplest mentalism mind reading tricks that always promises a good result using tarot cards.

The reader riffles quickly through the deck of cards and asks the subject to tell him when to stop. The subject then takes the card, not revealing it to the reader. The reader then gives a reading to the subject describing their personality and concludes by saying, *"based on that reading it is my guess that you would have pulled out the Ace of Cups. Am I right?"* Of course, that's what the reader is holding in their hand.

How the effect is done is incredibly simple. After shuffling the deck the reader glances at the very bottom card and then cuts the deck. He will place his little "pinky" finger slightly over the edge of the bottom half of the cut. This keeps the cut separated with the bottom card resting hidden on top of the little finger. He then riffles through the deck telling the subject to say "stop" at any time. When the subject says stop the reader quickly move the upper half of the deck forward and lifts it off revealing the card at the bottom of the cut that he glanced at before the cut (in magic this is referred to as a "card force," and there are hundreds of ways of doing them.)

When the reading is over and the reader "guesses" what card the subject "randomly" picked it will tend to verify that the reader is "the real deal," and thus make every other aspect of the reading true and acceptable.

The Seven Hidden Addictions

The seven hidden addictions are described by Blair Warren in his hard to find book "The Forbidden Keys of Persuasion." These "addictions" are simply things that everyone responds to.

A psychic can never fail by appealing to these powerful human needs. This is especially true of the addictions of **needing hope** and the need to have a **scapegoat**.

When it comes to needing hope you will never lose out by providing someone with hope during a psychic reading. You can give them cautions and let them know there are things they should pay attention to, but don't destroy their hope.

If there is a problem they are facing you will do best to find a way to let them know it is not their fault; give them a scapegoat. I don't recommend you tell them they've been cursed or anything like that. Instead, reassure them that they've done all they could and that they are a good person.

It is also a good idea to let the person know that they are in some way needed and important to the people around them.

If you are going to go into doing psychic cold readings make a point of reading and incorporating "**The Seven Hidden Addictions**" in your reading and people will naturally love what you tell them.

Training for Unconscious Response

To my knowledge, this trick is the first time it is been revealed in writing, but it is been alluded to by magicians who practice mind reading and mentalism tricks. Many psychic cold readers use it unconsciously with great effect. it is called the "eyebrow raise," using the raised eyebrow and head nod to get unconscious confirmation.

The reader starts by making asking a question that they know or strongly suspect that the subject will respond "yes." For example, noticing the watch on the right wrist the reader will ask in the tone of a statement, *"you seem like someone who looks at things a bit differently than others. You're left handed. Aren't you?"* The reader will raise the eyebrows and nod as if asking for confirmation. The subject will then respond. When they respond with a yes, they will also unconsciously nod their head to the eyebrow raise. This act begins to train them to respond with unconscious signals. When the answer to a statement asked in this manner is "no" they will pause, which allows the reader to backtrack.

Here is an example of "mind reading" done in this manner...

"I'd like to ask you to think of a memory. Make sure it is a pleasant memory that you remember from way back."

This directs the subject to go "way back" and find a pleasant memory. Already the memories are being limited by the reader. The reader will then direct the questions based on the subject's unconscious responses to the eyebrow raise and nod.

"This was a when you were young..." (eyebrow raise) *"....quite young"* (eyebrow raise, noting pause response) *"not too young...a teenage"* (subject gives an unconscious yes nod.) *"Okay, so you are a teenager. This is a special occasion...*(eyebrow raise and nod not noticing a response)*...it is not that special...it is a regular day but something nice is happening. You are with friends, family members* (notice whether they respond to "friends" or "family members.")

Mediumship and Group Reading

Mediumship is the art of working with people who want to speak with a dead friend of relative.

This does take some practice and experience to do well, but it is surprising how simple it can be. Many people will do a psychic reading for a group of people. The reader would start by reading "someone in the group" without being specific who it is. This makes it even easier because it is much easier to find someone who will agree that the reading applies to them. One such reading can be as follows...

"There is someone here who lost someone, a close friend or family member. The loss happened during a celebration or holiday...that's how you remember it."

During this open reading the reader would be looking around for signs of unconscious agreement. Then look at the person who is responding to what they say.

Many cold readings do not involve fishing, vagueness, or wild guessing. The key to a successful cold reading is the willingness, ability, and effort of the client to find meaning and significance in the words of the psychic, astrologer, palm reader, or medium. A medium claiming to get messages from the dead might throw out a string of ambiguous images to the client. *"Father figure, the month of May, the Big-H, and H with an N sound, Henna, Henry, M, maybe Michael, teaching, books, maybe something published."* This list could mean different things to different people. To some people it probably has no meaning. The client will either connect these dots or she won't.

Clients of mediums who claim to get messages from the dead are very highly motivated clients. Not only do they have an implicit desire for immortality, they have an explicit desire to contact a dear loved one who has died. The odds are in favor of the medium that the client will find meaning in many different sets of ambiguous words and phrases. If she connects just a couple of them, she may be satisfied that the medium has made a connection to a dead relative. If she doesn't find any meaning or significance in the string, the medium still wins. He can try another string. He can insist that there is meaning here but the client just isn't trying hard enough to figure it out. He can suggest that some uninvited spirit guests are confusing the issue. It's a win-win situation for the medium because the burden is not on him but on the client to find the meaning and significance of the words.

If you ever get a chance to see one of those psychic readers who tells people about their dead friends and relatives you will learn a lot about cold reading and working with unconscious responses.

Hellstromism

Hellstromism is a magic or mentalism process that comes about as close to actual psychic ability as is actually possibly.

The effect of Hellstromism is to ask a volunteer to either hide an object within a room or think of a location within the room. The psychic then has the volunteer take his wrist and, without speaking, begins walking and quickly finds the secret object or location.

Hellstromism originated from a performer calling himself "Alex Hellstrom, The Mindreader" who specialized in this type of demonstration.

The secret to success in this type of psychic demonstration depends upon how you instruct the volunteer to assist you and the degree of practice you've put behind you.

You will have asked your volunteer to hide an object in a room while you stand outside the room with the door closed. Preferably the room is a large room in which there are many hiding places. The object must NOT be hidden on a person or on themselves and must be in a stationary hiding place. When you start learning Hellstromism agree upon the object before hand. As your skill improves you can even instruct your volunteer to NOT tell you which object he or she has hidden.

Once they returned from hiding the object you give them your instruction.

Instructing The Volunteer

To do this effectively you have to clearly inform your volunteer what he or she must do. Let them know the success of this demonstration is reliant upon their ability to concentrate and think loudly in their minds the commands you will give them. The following monologue assumes you don't know what object is being hidden and it will go something like this...

"I am going to ask you to take my right wrist with your left hand (hold the right arm up for them to take and wait for them to grasp it)."

"As I enter the room, FOLLOW ME. Of course, I assume the experiment is to be concluded in this room (the volunteer may say 'yes' but caution him or her to not speak aloud – ONLY TO THINK THE WORDS unless requested to answer verbally.) Now, as we enter the room (you remain standing) you are FIRST to think of the location of the object. THINK to which part of the room to go."

"If the object is to your right, THINK TURN RIGHT (at this point you move your right arm to the right, indicating that direction) or if we are to turn left, THINK TURN LEFT (indicate by moving your arm to the left.) When we come to the proper location, THINK STOP (you now draw up your hands, fists clasped tightly in a manner similar to pulling in the reins of a horse.) When we are in the proper location say to yourself – THAT'S RIGHT, NOW BEND OVER AND TAKE THE OBJECT (force down with the hands.) BUT should I take the wrong object, say to yourself NO NO THAT'S WRONG PUT IT BACK (move the hands back.) Do you understand? When I find the selected article say, YES THAT'S RIGHT now turn to your right or left, whichever the case may be (demonstrate) and when I have come to the proper location the second time, just repeat over and over again in your mind the command. Concentrate, step by step, and WHEREVER I go, right or wrong, YOU FOLLOW ME! But concentrate. Are your ready? (act as if you are ready to bolt, eager and fidgety, you want to get to it.)

"LET'S GO!"

At this point you will find most good subjects start to walk directly toward the object and it's hiding place. You can use this by, instead of taking that first step, feign by raising to your toes and lean forward so the subject is likely to take the first step before you...and not notice it. They will very likely indicate the direction you are to go.

Because of how you instructed the subject you will feel a slight tug or pull at those moments they are thinking of the directions. This is all unconscious on their part but at times you'll notice them pulling on your arm as if they were guiding you.

Know What Your Subject Thinks, For Real

If you know something about NLP (Neuro Linguistic Programming), you've no doubt heard of eye-accessing cues. These are the movement your eyes make when you are thinking, and especially when you've been asked a question.

When someone asks us a question, and we don't know the answer right off the bat, we will often move our eyes to "access" this information in our brains.

Generally speaking when you are looking at someone and you ask that person a question, his or her eyes will move up and towards the (your) right when they are visually remembering something, the eyes will move towards your left when they are creating something or thinking about the future.

Now if their eyes move towards the sides (on level with their ears), they are hearing something internally. If his or her eyes move towards your right, they are remembering something they heard and if their eyes move towards your left, they are thinking of what someone will say in the future.

As you are giving a reading, keep an eye on your sitter's eyes. If they move up and towards the side ask them what they saw or are seeing. If they move towards the side, ask them what they heard or are hearing inside.

You can comment based on their eye accessing cues. When done well it can seem to the reader that you are indeed reading their mind. Examples of what to say are given with the illustrations below.

Of course, your sitters won't be aware of what you're doing and will be baffled at how you can know HOW they are thinking.

There's a lot more on eye-accessing cues than I can give here. Almost any book that teaches NLP will show you how to master this reading skill.

So can the direction a person's eyes reveal whether or not they are making a truthful statement?

The Short Answer: *sort of.*

Reading people's minds isn't as simple as some recent television shows or movies make it seem.

In these shows a detective will deduce whether or not a person is being truthful simply because they looked to the left or right while making a statement. In reality, it would be foolish to make such a snap judgment without further investigation...but the technique does have some merit. So, here it is...read, ponder and test it on your friends and family to see how reliable it is for yourself.

Visual Accessing Cues

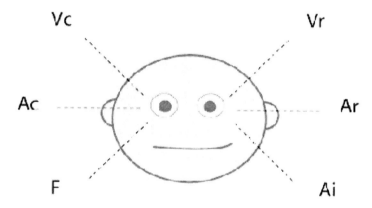

The first time "Visual Accessing Cues" were discussed (at least to my knowledge) was by Richard Bandler and John Grinder in their book "Frogs into Princes: Neuro Linguistic Programming (NLP)" From their experiments this is what they found...

When asked a question a "normally organized" right-handed person looks (from your viewpoint, looking at them):

Up and to the Left

This motion indicates **visually *constructed* images (Vc).** If you asked someone to "imagine a purple buffalo," this would be the direction their eyes moved in while thinking about the question as they visually constructed a purple buffalo in their mind.

If you see this at the time of the reading you might say, *"a person very naturally wonders about how these ideas would look and how best to make these pictures so pleasant that they feel good, certain and inevitable."*

Up and to the Right

Looking up and to the right indicates **visually remembered** images **(Vr).** If you asked someone "what color was the first house you lived in?" this would be the direction the average right-handed person would move their eyes while thinking about the question. They are visually remembering the color of their childhood home.

When seeing this during a cold reading you can comment:

"Thinking back to those images can, in their own way give you a sense of comfort or a reminder that what you remember learning from that experience is still with you and there to help you."

To the Left

This motion indicates **auditory *constructed* (Ac)** thoughts. If you asked someone to "try and create the highest pitched sound possible in your head" then this would be the direction their eyes would move in while thinking about the question. They are auditorily constructing this sound in their head that they have never heard before.

"Perhaps you're trying to imagine a sound or conversation that gives you the encouragement you want and need. At these times I advise that you make the words and sounds as positive and supportive as you might imagine them. Full, rich, resonating through you."

To the Right

Looking sideways and to the right likely signifies **auditory *remembered* (Ar)** thoughts. If you asked someone to "remember what their mother's voice sounds like," this would be the direction their eyes moved in while thinking about the question as they auditorily remembered this sound.

"You can remember the sound of _____ and how it affected you. Let those sounds be supportive and positive of everything you want to do so that even now as you remember them they encourage you to move on."

Down and to the Left

This look indicated **Feeling / Kinesthetic (F)** mental activity. If you asked someone to "can you remember the smell of a campfire?" this would be the direction their eyes moved in while thinking about the question as they used recalled a smell, feeling, or taste.

"You might be feeling moved or touched by a feeling that has it's own personal meaning to you in this reading. It's important to use those feeling positively without having to linger on them. Do we agree?"

Down and to the Right

This motion indicates an **internal dialog (Ai).** This is the direction of someone eyes as they "talk to themselves."

"Regardless of what you tell yourself right now it's possible to search inside and find a deeper meaning to every part of this reading."

Final Notes On Eye Cues

– Looking straight ahead or with eyes that are defocused and unmoving is also considered a sign of visual accessing.

– A typical left-handed person would have the opposite eye-accessing cues.

– As with other signs of lying, you should first establish and understand a person's baseline behavior before concluding they are lying by the direction of their eyes.

– Many critics believe the above is a bunch of bullshit. In my own experiments I have found these techniques to be more true than not. But, why not find out for yourself? Make up a list of questions that are like the sample ones and give them to your friends, family, or anyone who would be your guinea pig. Observe their eye movements and record the results.

When Magic Happens

I was doing a tarot reading for a young woman at a street fair. She was with her mother and a friend.

The reading was going as usual when it came to the topic of relationships and she stopped me and asked about how her relationship with her sister will transpire. At that moment I looked her straight in the eye and said "you're an identical twin and you and your sister had a falling out."

The young woman's jaw dropped and she looked at her mother who shared her amazement. Somehow I had hit the nail squarely on the head.

I gave her some advice about how to deal with her sister...which I no longer remember...and assured her things would work out.

Months later I heard from her telling me that things transpired just as I had predicted.

Famed actor Orson Welles was also a well practiced magician and cold reader. In an interview he began to describe how, after a day of doing readings, a woman came into the room and as the reading began he blurted out "you recently lost your husband." she instantly burst into tears.

It was true.

As you go about using the cold reading skills that you've learned it is very likely that some very strange things will happen where you say or know things that you truly have no right nor reason of knowing. These events will be highlights of what seem to be real psychic phenomenon. I can say that yes, they do happen.

People take up the skill of cold reading for all sorts of reasons, to meet girls, to impress people, to make money. Even if you are a complete skeptic to psychic ability it is very likely that you will have several of those moments of lucid insight that impress both you and your client. These are moments that we cold readers live for, yet they defy reason.

Two questions arise from these wondrous events. How does this take place? How can I make this happen more often?

I would like to try to address both these questions based on my own personal experience. Please keep in mind that all of this is my own highly biased view of how the mind works.

How does this take place?

The best answer to this question has come to me from my intense study and application of neuro-linguistic programming (NLP for short). A huge portion of NLP is devoted to the topic of rapport.

Rapport is that "magical connection" that occurs when we are with people whom we share certain commonalities. When rapport is good we feel comfortable and responsive to one another. When the rapport is strong we find ourselves matching each others mood and emotions. We may even find ourselves finishing the other person's sentence as if our minds were synced in unison.

With rapport anything is possible. Without rapport it is like speaking to an angry wall and nothing is possible.

It is therefore no surprise that these strange psychic events will happen most often when you are in deep rapport with your client.

There is another factor that is more akin to the preternatural than the mechanical act of cold reading. It is the reader's use of intuition.

Let's face it. Intuition is not always rational. Intuition is a wondrous ability that everyone possesses, to a more or less degree, and it can be developed with practice. Intuition will develop with the ongoing practice of cold reading.

Perhaps intuition is simply a keener sense of observation and an understanding of certain situations in life, but I cannot say for sure.

Regardless, believing you have intuition is nothing unless you are willing to test it. Don't confuse your imagination with your intuition. This means testing the things you intuit for accuracy.

You will find that it cannot always be turned on like a light switch but that it does exist. By testing your intuition you learn to better trust your hunches.

Now we come to the second question, the question that you hope will help turn you into a real life psychic.

How can I make this happen more often?

Let's admit it now, practicing something is a conscious effort and it means putting aside the time, thought and the focus to get something done.

What I'm going to suggest are a few very useful exercises that should help you bring intuition into a more helpful role as you do cold readings.

Step 1 – Build Rapport

As mentioned in the previous pages rapport has a powerful effect on how we understand and influence people.

There are many ways to build rapport, and if you want to know all of them you can spend a couple of hundred buck on NLP books and training.

If you want to learn to create rapport quickly...dare I say it...instantly, then the next paragraph will save you a load of money.

To create powerful and instant rapport the key is simple: assume you already have it. That means that even if you have never met your client before that moment you should create a feeling within yourself that you already know and like them. In fact, imagine the feeling of them being a long lost old friend that you haven't seen in years, and treat them accordingly (don't be too eager; you don't want to freak them out.)

I once knew a man who could gain rapport the moment he met you. As soon as he met you he would shout out your name as if he hadn't seen you in ages. His greetings were so sincere and welcoming you couldn't help but feel a connection with him.

Step 2 – Imagine Being Them

I am constantly amazed at how much POWERFUL information one can learn by taking a moment to imagine being in the other person's body...literally.

This can all be done very quickly if you put aside your own assumptions and prejudices about other people for a moment and imagine what it's like to live in their body. The range of insights about them can range from physical aches and pains to recent emotional heartaches and even an awareness of their fears and insecurities.

When doing this in a reading it's a good idea to hedge your bets by being vague about these insights.

Step 3 – Hellstromism

Whenever you get a chance to practice hellstromism then do it. If you're new to it then just practice it as a fun experiment with friends.

Practicing it will sharpen your awareness about how people send unconscious signals.

Step 4 – Trust Your Unconscious

It is your unconscious mind that gives you these intuitions. For many people the unconscious minds gives only vague "gut feelings" as to what to do. As a cold reader who relies on intuition you will need to open up a broader dialogue with the unconscious mind to enlist its help.

This exercise may seem strange, even insane, but it has been instrumental in getting those "gut feelings" to come about more quickly.

The exercise is a simple one-sided but respectful petition to the unconscious mind for help. It consists of three parts: an apology, a promise, and gratitude.

It sounds something like this...

"Unconscious Mind, I want to apologize for not paying attention to you when you've wanted my attention. I promise that from this point on I will acknowledge you and your 'gut feelings' and intuitions when they come about. Thank you, Unconscious Mind, for being there for me. I deeply appreciate how you have helped and supported me."

Seriously, by giving your unconscious mind the type of respect that anyone would appreciate you'll find that it will begin to do for you what it was meant to do; help you without having to think.

Step 5 – Exercise Your Intuition

As mentioned earlier when you use your intuition you should also test it to see if it's a hit or miss.

A very fun and simple game you can play is to find a person you do not know, but may have a reason to talk to, a store clerk or checkout person, for example. Before you speak to them go through the rapport exercises mentioned in this section and ask yourself a few simple questions that they might be able to confirm or deny.

A good example of this is to try to intuit the name of one of their close friends. Then when you meet them (perhaps as they check out your groceries) you can ask them *"do you know a person named _____?"*

They either do or they don't, and you will instantly have tested your intuition.

Regardless of how they answer you can simply pass off your question by saying, "I thought I might have met you through someone I know," or "I keep thinking I might know your friend…maybe I'm wrong. Thanks!"

Since you don't know them you can simply leave and let them go on with their business. If you find them interesting you can always devise a way to continue the conversation.

Final Thoughts

As mentioned at the beginning of this book, cold reading is at best an art form that starts off as a science. There is no real end to what you can learn about cold reading, and it's likely that most of what you will learn about cold reading will happen from doing it.

I would like to conclude this book with a few words of advice and encouragement.

So…

You can use cold reading for all sorts of reasons. To meet and get to know attractive women, to earn money, to get some recognition and fame.

Regardless of your reasons I HIGHLY encourage you to be NICE with your readings. While you may emphasize that readings are for "entertainment purposes only" don't be surprised that people will take your words VERY seriously…often as a matter of life and death. That means doing what you can to have people leave your session feeling better then when they entered.

In the short run you could exploit people's fears and desires and earn a bit of change. In the long run it will probably not help you. So have a bigger picture in mind and do whatever you can to help people with your skills.

Oh, yeah. Don't forget to have fun!

All the best,

Dantalion Jones

9 780578 044644